WELCOME TO A DAILY CELEBRATION!

*A DAILY CELEBRATION is a One-of-a-Kind Interactive Journal comprised
of 365 Original Daily quotes written by Author Joslin Fitzgerald,
also known as
Publisher Mary Fitzgerald Joslin.*

*When you buy A DAILY CELEBRATION you
essentially receive Four books in one!
In that delightful statement with everybody appreciating being
given something extra. You will See by using the specially
provided QR CODES found inside this Exclusive Book,
that this Directional Journal will take you to many Merry Places!
In that exciting transfer you will enjoy reading some of the Authors' other writing.*

*So, wanting you to own a Fun, Insightful, likewise Unique Daily Inspirational
Journal that will help you find the best things about time. In that line of
progression, you will like following the seasons as this book highlights the
Holidays, while… A DAILY CELEBRATION helps guide your life.*

*Therefore, shore to shore, the world over,
on the promise that this writing will help to make your life better!
A DAILY CELEBRATION will inspire you to find
the Comfort, and Hope you are missing.
And as these rejuvenating ideas, and renewing thoughts assist you in finding the
Individual Guidance you are seeking.
You will further discover the Daily Encouragement,
also, Enlightenment that you need!
Then in those Personal Life Changing Discoveries
you will realize that the Private Insight found on these beautiful pages,
will take you to your own
DAILY
CELEBRATION.*

*This book is dedicated to my family who continues to love and support me.
Thank you John, Ryan, Baby Love,
Adam, Ailee, Aria, Victoria,
John Mark, Amanda, Olivia, Emma,
Jimmy, Rebecca, Kendall,
Peter, Joy, Zachary, Preston, also Ryan…..
for always being there for me*

JANUARY

Joslinfitzgerald.com

To find the EXCITING SURPRISES waiting inside, Click
on the QR CODES that have been provided.
There you will see that these lighthouse guides will take you where you need to go!

1. *To start the New year right leave the past behind. Leaving the past behind, keep moving on with time. Then knowing the best has yet to arrive, the future will greet you, as you look forward to a happier life.*

2. *To wipe the slate clean don't bring the old fear of the past into your New Year. To start over celebrate everything! And as you erase the pain and uncertainty of yesterday, embrace the hope today brings.*

3. *As the old year dies, and New Year arrives, knowing everything can change in one day or night. Do not mourn what you left behind. But instead find peace and commencement in the mornings light.*

4. *The future's message in a New Year's Kiss will always be found in its intent. That's why, to begin again, you need to kiss the old off, and one more time, kiss the sweet celebration of the New Year in!*

5. *Since things will never be as bad as they seem why are you crying? Tears never accomplish anything. But a positive uplifting attitude will change everything! So, to make the New Year Happy start smiling!*

6. *To keep the party going you need to know if the celebration is stopping or starting. To have a Happy New Year, also to keep Celebrating everything, seek what will fulfill you. Find what makes you Happy!*

7. *In the New Year Kiss Off, you must know why everything needs to change. So, to Kiss Off the mess in the past Close the door on yesterday, lock the latch on depression, end anxiety, and Stop your stress.*

8. *There can't be a Happily-Ever-After if what comes after is not happy. And you can't be happy if you are not filled with hope. So, for a new resolution find the future, and the plans that will help you cope.*

9. *Don't go backwards! But in redirection of resolutions go forward. Hang on. Don't fall apart. Leave troubles behind. Find your promise tomorrow, and that decision will lead you to the best part of life.*

10. *Are you bringing an old broken heart into the new year? With fear staying near are you afraid that pain will not go away. If so leave your faulty heart behind and look for the difference you need to find.*

11. *Time will mend your fractures, but only harmony and love can Start a broken heart. So, to find the calm that will not depart. In your New Year leave the worry of your past behind and make a fresh start.*

12. *To avoid the frightful black ice of life watch where you are going. To stand when you are falling, as you keep things from slipping away, be safe from injury by finding firm footing on solid ground today.*

13. *A wish that doesn't exist can't hold a candle to hope, and anticipation that will be there. So, to find the delight in life never rely on an empty wish or unkept resolution, to bring you a Happy New Year.*

14. *In some ways All days are the same. That means every day can be a Birthday, Present, or Holiday! So, take the best of the day, send sorrow away, and know there will always be something To Celebrate!*

15. *Pain ignores time. But time heals pain! So, if you have great pain you can't ignore or explain, know the nights and days will dry your old tears, and time will rebuild you, as you begin a Happy New Year.*

16. *Don't live in yesterday's devastation. Instead put your past depression, stress, problems, and messes behind you. Then finding your happiness in today, a great new peaceful future will come your way.*

17. *Whether it's cold outside, or hot as Hell day or night, by looking at life differently and turning your back on worry. As you keep smiling, and chill out, you will eventually find that everything is alright!*

18. *Life will never be black or white, because there will always be something unseen in-between. That means if you want to be happy, concentrate on the best life brings, and ignore negativity you can feel.*

19. *As the old year dies, and New Year arrives time flies by. To enjoy that time, leave the past and black ice behind and following the cool plans for your future you will find the best in the days and nights.*

20. *The light is stronger than the darkness inside of you. So, as the light shines to keep the darkness from overtaking you, know there will always be something delightful to hold onto and see every day.*

21. *To stop the wreck, obey the light! And going the right direction in life by doing things the safe way, put your troubles behind. Then surviving the breakdown, blow out, and crash, you will enjoy the ride!*

22. *Wrecks hurt your heart and neck. So, be careful where you head. To guard your insides and protect your outsides on the drive through life follow the signs by obeying lights that are yellow, green and red.*

23. *To survive the end of the 911 line likewise, to endure the Scary wrecks in time change what is wrong also frightening. So, knowing where you need to be going, start heading the right way in your life!*

24. *At the edge of Deadly Cliff with you ready to jump you must know how to stop slipping. In that cliff hanger test. Step back, find control, then your footing and balance will get you where you need to go.*

25. *Do not trust your future to fake wishes. Instead seek your bliss where blessings exist. And finding a way to forgive those who hurt you. To guard your heart, don't let fear, anger, or revenge rip you apart.*

26. *To have everything you need know things will get better. To end pain, keep healing and breathing. To see beauty around you by trusting in the future, you will find the comfort and sweet relief you need.*

27. *In the winter of life to stop crying about your problems, face your troubles. To get where you want to be, start thinking about things in a different way. Then by solving your anxiety, you will find peace.*

28. *To survive the dark times don't be blind. Open your eyes! Don't be worried or blindsided. Instead, find a safe place where tears no longer exist in your heart or mind, by turning your back on your fears.*

29. *To keep breathing find your reason for living. To be rescued, find a way to escape your grief. To find your heart's desire start smiling. Next to find your nice purpose in life... you need to stop crying.*

30. *To see the reason for change, you must know why things need to be renewed. To not waste time in the night or day you need to realize that change can be a good thing in life. So let change, Change you!*

31. *Fears and tears will Not accomplish anything. A tear makes everything dark as night. Crying is also a waste of time! But a bright outlook will bring smiles, blue skies, and delightful things into your life!*

FEBRUARY

Joslinfitzgerald.com

*To find the EXCITING SURPRISES waiting inside, Click
on the QR CODES that have been provided.
There you will see that these lighthouse guides will take you where you need to go!*

1. *To celebrate Valentine's day all the time don't depend on things in your sight. Instead, look for the things you don't see with your eyes. And as you open your eyes to love, that's how to protect your heart.*

2. *Big scary days will get better when problems become smaller. So, to reduce your stress, find your guidance inside your mind. Don't get overwhelmed by time because no misery is as big as your life.*

3. *People are like ground hogs they are wrong, right, or undecided. To find out which one you will be, make your choice. Then knowing the Difference between wrong and right you will never be indecisive.*

4. *Going down life's track, I love you means nothing unless somebody says it back. To find the I love you and loving guiding affection also joy that has come to stay, tell somebody… you love them today.*

5. *It's about time. It's also about love and life. So, to make the most of time, Enjoy life. Then finding someone you can be kind to right now, by helping them out, you will share your love in a grateful way.*

6. *In life no matter the reason or season… peace, love, and freedom are everything! That's why, to be happy day and night you must agree some of the great things in life will always be found in these three.*

7. *Let's think about sweet things that will take you in the right direction. Then thinking that way it will always be important to listen to and follow your heart, after all, your heart knows the right way to start!*

8. *To know why good or bad things happen in your life, you need to know the reason for them. Because as things bless your heart, or slice it apart, the sweet and sour things in time will all play a giant part.*

9. *Life will not be a piece of cake. So, if you don't like seeing your sour history replace your nice future. Turn your back on your embittered past. Next to enjoy your piece of cake. Change your future fast.*

10. *To keep a heart from breaking you need to keep it safe also uncut. This is important, because if you take care of people and their hearts, they won't be broken, and you won't break down, or break apart.*

11. *To play the game of life right, you must know what side you are on. Then being on the right team, while making the right decisions you can succeed in your overtime exciting game, that you are playing.*

12. *Are the games in life that you play important? Or is it more important how you play the game? That all depends on what games you are playing. And if you have the balls to play, also to win the game.*

13. *In life's game is it better to be an offensive or defensive player? That depends on what game you play. So, for things to keep working, follow your plan. Be on the right team. Then Go win the game.*

14. *Will Valentine's Day find you sadly alone or knowing you are never alone will you be happy at home? To be happy wherever you go, find the sweet, loving song in your heart that will not depart.*

15. *When the game is over, will you win or lose? Remember even if you lose. Play to win. Don't lose the game by not enjoying the day. That's important since Losers will always be winners in their own way.*

16. *Losing your marbles, do you have any balls? That all depends on if you are going crazy in isolation, or knowing you are never alone, are you happy at home with what you are doing, also who you are.*

17. *So blows the old cold winter's wind. But that's okay. Don't worry about things that are out of your control. By trusting life will get better, you know that the spring of contentment will be coming again.*

18. *If you are not happy, you are like a frozen rose. Because when a rose freezes nothing will grow. But when you nourish it with the sun of happiness, that's when life, hope, and the rose will start to unfold.*

19. *The difference between a dying rose and one growing on the vine, is what is inside. So, to find the strength you need to get through life, hold on tight and look for beauty, also purpose in your time.*

20. *Walking through a Frightening tornado in life is never easy. But as you witness its power, and pick up the pieces from its devastation, you will be stronger after Surviving the hail, flood, and lightning.*

21. *To have Valentine's day every night you must find peace inside. Next to bless your heart you need to find somebody who will always love you. Yes, find somebody to trust, who will not tear your life apart.*

22. *A cold dark heart will never grow. But a rose that finds its light will never die. So, to protect your life as you achieve your happiness find something to be grateful for and leave your darkness behind.*

23. *To give a gift of love and light share your heart from the start. Then disclosing the experiences of your life by finding the wisdom and insight attached to your history, you will discover who you are.*

24. *To find the light and happiness in life, turn away from your sadness and problems that are making you cry. To find the rainbows delight inside your eyes, look for the good things that make you smile.*

25. *To stay away from the termination found in a mental deadly hibernation, Wake up. Next to leave your dark surrendering*

thoughts behind you, fill your excited mind with rejuvenating directing ideas.

26. *To unlock the perplexing secrets that you keep hiding, bring them into the light. Then facing your troubles and pain today Open your eyes. It's better to face the facts, than keep them locked up inside.*

27. *To understand what's going on you need to know the answers to the solutions that you are seeking. To discover the key resolutions, find the people in life who know Why you are asking the big questions.*

28. *If you want to stay forever young, stay young forever in your mind and heart. In life everyone gets old, some older. But, to stay young inside, you need to stop feeling tired, also old and stop falling apart!*

(29.) *Is it better to be a weed or a flower? Keep in mind a fragile flower will give up and die. But a weed will fight for its life, while finding its renewed strength inside, as it stays alive. So, when You feel like a weed that's alright, because that's when you will find the strength you need to survive your hard times!*

February's Surprise Writing. In life have you ever questioned what season you are in? Then feeling like it will always be wintertime inside your mind. Being weak when you need to be strong, have you ever felt like a rose that won't grow? Well knowing at times, you will feel like a dying rose. Stop thinking that way! Because you Cannot be weak when you need to be strong. Likewise, you cannot die inside if you want to find the best things in life. So, to be Strong… When You Cannot be Weak, be Courageous when you feel Discouraged. Then like a rose growing and sleeping below the snow, you will realize no matter what time or season it is in your life, since you found your strength within; you will always be like a rose coming alive in the early spring!

MARCH

Joslinfitzgerald.com

To find the EXCITING SURPRISES waiting inside, Click
on the QR CODES that have been provided.
There you will see that these lighthouse guides will take you where you need to go!

1. *To wake up before it's too late face the dawn of a new day. And to find the beginning of a great new spring, surround yourself with things and caring people who give you purpose, insight, also clarity.*

2. *Inside every old person is a young person who is living their life. And as the future comes alive that means there is a wise person gaining insight who is quite young in their mind, still enjoying the ride.*

3. *To survive life's disasters find what matters! To find what matters remember all things are directing your time. So, to make sure you have a nice happy ever after, always have a good day and sweet night.*

4. *If you go the wrong way, there will Not be a happily ever after. So, think carefully about where you are heading, and what you want to do. Then when you do it, find the plan that helps see you through.*

5. *How many disasters are coming? And in arriving trouble what will it take to climb out of the rubble? To answer those questions and survive depression, you must face your mess, and end your old stress.*

6. *To find Happily Ever After you need to survive the destruction also disasters, as you concentrate on what matters. Don't let the big or tiny destroying things take away the delight you are trying to find.*

7. *Most dreams survive, some die. That depends on if you keep hope alive or give up on what makes you come alive. So, trust your survival instincts, fulfill your dreams, and Celebrate All the days in-between!*

8. *Are you going into terrifying times? Are you afraid to face the day? Has, fear taken your joy away? If so, turn your back on what you dread. Then the worrying frustrating part of your future will disappear.*

9. *To know when chaos is over, you need to know when things are finished. When things are through you need to know when you begin again that the worst of the un-Known confusion will be over soon.*

10. *Seeing gives insight through the years. Using your ears means you are listening to what you need to hear. To listen to your heart, while seeing the path clearly, you are going the right way from the start.*

11. *Do you need to plot every part of your life, or is it okay to trust things will take care of themselves in some way? To find peace, turn loose of the reigns. Trust your decisions. Live your day by having faith.*

12. *It's nice to look forward to the good times that will arrive. So, to find out what time it is, by finding the delights in life, concentrate on the right hand of the clock and leave the sad left-over things behind.*

13. *Are you sick and tired worrying love will never stay. If so, know unless you open your heart and trust, love will never come your way. You must first love, to be loved. So, find a love that will remain.*

14. *Is the beginning better than the ending? Wondering which is better don't concentrate on the stops or starts of your heart, because it's what happens In-between, that will keep things from falling apart.*

15. *Are you looking for magic that does not exist? Or are you trusting in what is real? Never trusting in magic wishes, while enjoying what's true, find your fantasy, in your reality, which will transform you.*

16. Abracadabra, and presto change-o Opens nothing. On the other hand, opening your own doors will make sure that you put your unrealistic wishes away, while enjoying the sweet reality of your day.

17. Should all your dreams come true? Because not all dreams are good for you. So, knowing some dreams can be nightmares in disguise, don't be disappointed, if things go a different way in your life.

18. To be full of it is a good thing, if you are full of tranquility, goodwill, and sweet dreams. So, leave your troubles, questions, and uncertainties in the past. Think things through, do what completes you.

19. Can you find a pot of gold if there is no rainbow? In life don't go looking for a pot of gold or for wealth untold. Instead enjoy the blessings coming after the rain, located in the splendor of your goals.

20. After the tornado blows, look for the rainbow. Knowing rejuvenation comes after devastation by not fearing the pain, find something good in your day. Then great rebuilding things will come your way.

21. Since all roses have thorns, does that mean all dollars should have warnings? Remember things in this world will hurt you! But the safe, healing things found in your life's garden will never harm you.

22. To see the restoration an endless spring brings start growing within. To not run out of time seek the way to be released from hurt in your life. Then finding your smile, leave the bad and sad things behind.

23. Like a rose needs sunshine and water to flourish you also need truth to grow and shine. That's why you must know, if you live a life full of lies and gloom, you will never prosper, develop, glow, or bloom.

24. Below the snow a rose will grow. So, even though your plans are cold. Like the frozen rose they are waiting for you to wake up. So, don't give up on dreams that will always be sleeping... below the snow.

25. *To see the light and find your sight know that you are doing something right. To seek your refuge, capability, likewise protection, realize that you are making the right decision that will revive your life.*

26. *Time changes in the blink of an eye. That's why to survive the blind seasons that redo everything in sight, you must appreciate living. So, enjoy your renovation that will transform you into someone new.*

27. *To get to the ending, you must survive the middle. To start over at the beginning, leave past times behind. To appreciate life, enjoy the half time, and take care of the little things in-between the lines.*

28. *Life will always be a stormy ride. So, to find a way to stand up to the wild winds of time passing by, be strong. Knowing a calming tide is coming your way, do not give into fear today. Don't be afraid!*

29. *In the procession of time wars, storms, anxiety, disease, violence, fire, and misery will all be part of life. But finding the courage to survive pain, that's where your bravery, bliss, and strength will begin!*

30 *If you share good news, good news will come to you. So, to find your good news do not be troubled. Do not go looking for problems. Instead, by spreading good news look forward to what is coming soon.*

31. *For good news and great advice, if there is No music sing and smile! Stop crying and start dancing. Next to make yourself happy, revise what makes you sad, and as you sing, nothing will make you mad.*

March's Surprise Writing. To find gladness in your heart, you need to make sure peace never departs. To be whole inside your soul you must trust that things will get better in every way, by finding the happiness that stays. So, to be peaceful, happy, and whole don't let the pain of yesterday take away the hope of your today, or the promise of your tomorrow.

APRIL

Joslinfitzgerald.com

*To find the EXCITING SURPRISES waiting inside, Click
on the QR CODES that have been provided.
There you will see that these lighthouse guides will take you where you need to go!*

1. Do not act foolishly. So, Not wanting every day to be April fools, to make sure the joke is not on you. To end your doom, gloom, and unwise ways, find truth and certainty in what you are doing and saying.

2. To be fool proof don't play a fool. Instead, put foolish ideas behind you and find wisdom by listening to your heart talk. Don't be fooled by those who don't support you. Don't ever give up on you!

3. The rain grows flowers. So, like a spring seed receiving strength from the nourishing storm. As you survive the wild ride and understand what you have gone through you will bloom into a beautiful weed.

4. To find enchantment of a new spring know the true beauty and the endless possibilities a renewing season provides. To be on the right side of things, realize every day is a time to expand your horizons.

5. If you only wait for spring, you will be ignoring the life changing possibilities that the other seasons bring. So, to not miss a thing, open your eyes to the inside and outside beauty that will make you sing.

6. Is it fool's gold? Do you know the difference between truth and lies? To know what is real or fake in life, you need to See the difference before it's too late, while finding the truth, waiting inside your eyes.

7. *Fooling around is okay, if you know what you are doing. So, if you are a child playing games that's fine. But growing up needing to move on, you must know when to stop playing foolish games with time.*

8. *To play like a child dance through life! That's survival advice, since being an adult is hard! That's why to find an escape and release pain. You need to seek your inner child who will always want to play.*

9. *A frozen rose dies on the vine. But the rose of happiness, love, and friendship will grow for all time. So, don't waste time withering inside, instead come alive. Love, take chances, and find delight in life.*

10. *Time is full of thorns. But soon there will be an end to the stabbed hurt. So, leave behind the prickly pain in the past, ignore the thorns, put a plaster-cast on unhappiness, and trust the healing that lasts.*

11. *For things to come up roses, know what's planted in your garden. To keep away the dark doubts of weakness, know what you are growing, and plant things that bring you confidence, also self-assurance.*

12. *To survive winters cold, it is good to know that below the snow a rose is growing. So, remember even when things get hard the best is yet to come, and in your heart you will find harmony as you go along.*

13. *Love and a rose need the same thing to survive. They both need someone to support and believe in them. So don't give up on love or the rose, and as they grow they each will bring beauty into your life.*

14. *To survive the thorns and storms of time, find a way to see through strife. Next, to end your fears, and pass your depressing scary tests get some rest. Then being rested you will finally see things clearly.*

15. *Your heart will die if you serve it alibis or lies. But your heart will be healthy and released if you feed it truth and peace. So, make sure things you say and do bless your heart then enjoy your new start.*

16. At the end of a storm the rainbow means something new is coming. So, Don't fear the hail! Then releasing the pain of change look forward to the exciting transformation the rainbow brings your way.

17. To survive storms in life, stay away from what brings tears to your eyes. To stop tears, see clearly. Next, to find the shelter and required protection you need, seek happiness, and quiet inside your mind.

18. Even if you can't see it, since it faded away, a rainbow tells us everything is okay. So, when you are in a storm to survive the pain even if your rainbow evaporated just know something better is on its way.

19. A tornado of the heart is worse than one in a park. That's why to survive the frightening storms that rip your life apart, take cover from the rain's pain by facing fear with hope, as you guard your heart.

20. If you ignore the storm warnings in life you will run into trouble, and out of time. That's why, to survive the wild rides and make the most of life, listen to the warnings to find your fortification in life.

21. If you think the tornado will miss you, you won't be ready for the Blow arriving. In life you will be Hit by a Tornado of Fear and Pain. That's why to protect yourself you must know a storm is on its way.

22. To survive a tornado of the heart find a safe place to hide. So, before the scary funnel of fear rips you apart find tranquility in your mind. Next locate your heart's armor in someone you love, also like.

23. To survive a hurricane of pain, you need to find the reason for the hail and rain. So, knowing that we need thunderstorms to grow, stop fearing your storms, and start looking forward to your rainbows!

24. To find your way out of the funnel climb over the rubble. To survive the devastation of the tornado, as you put your days back together you need to pick up the missing parts of your life, home, and heart.

25. *You can't depend on weather, life, love, or time so why do you plan your day around them? Instead, don't worry about the crazy things arriving you can't fix, and depend on the things you can manage.*

26. *As days flip and shift weather will switch. So, to survive a hurricane or tornado of time, remember once you pick up the pieces, and leave the old struggles and damage behind, you can have a better life.*

27. *There's a lot of talk about bombs, coughs, fires, tornados, hurricanes, fires, viruses, and other awful stuff. So, to Survive things that will hurt you look forward to nice things that will not wreck your heart.*

28. *Is the beginning the ending? Or is the end a beginning? That depends on which way you are going. So, to find the best of both, think carefully about what you are saying, doing, needing, and wanting.*

29. *To permanently exit means you won't be allowed to enter again. So, at your new Beginning to find a song in your heart know whether things are stopping or starting before they break your thoughts apart.*

30. *Something big will arrive. That's why, to find good things in life that will excite you as you protect your heart from what will tear it apart, open your eyes to the promise something awesome is coming.*

April's Surprise Writing. Wanting to send you a message that will bring peace to your life.. have you ever listened to the gentle song in the wind? And knowing listening to the friendly song in the wind will always be a comforting thing. To take a mental vacation from your life, you need to realize that listening to the wind will always be a great way to take a rest from your tests, stress, problems, and depression. Yes that's nice to know, because the message of hope found in the gentle song of the wind, will give you a mental break…as it tells you every day…to calm your mind, you need to look for your peace inside that you need to find.

MAY

Joslinfitzgerald.com

*To find the EXCITING SURPRISES waiting inside, Click
on the QR CODES that have been provided.
There you will see that these lighthouse guides will take you where you need to go!*

1. To keep things from blowing away hold on tight to what remains. Life will be a frightening wild ride. That's why to find Good in goodbye, you need to welcome the delightful times that will make you smile.

2. To see the good Leaving brings. Find the Good in goodbye by changing the bad things that make you sick and cringe. Then saying Hi to the mornings light, you will find the good in your days and nights.

3. Beauty in life will be seen yet its presence will be fleeting. So, with things evaporating in front of your eyes. Know it is more important to be beautiful Inside your heart than outside on the other parts.

4. Are you an unwanted weed in a rose garden? Do you feel ugly outside? Well don't worry about what you see. Instead, to find the beauty in life, today and tomorrow, care more about how you are growing.

5. Are your life and nest a mess? Are you living with depression? Are you under stress? If so you need to take a break from your mess, stress, and depression. Next to clean up life, decontaminate your mind.

6. *To get an A on a paper means you learned something. So, to pass life's 101 test keep studying. More exams are coming. That's why commencement and graduation will always be critical to your success.*

7. *A choice made is a decision that changes everything. Therefore, to Never close the wrong door, you need to make the right choice today. Then passing the tests that correct decision will lessen your stress.*

8. *In commencement time, make up your mind. Choices need to be made. But remember all choices will make, break, or change a day. So, think it through then make the most of the options coming for you.*

9. *To survive yesterday's fear, you need to graduate. And as you find the redirection of today that will lead to your goals, you will know that the promise of tomorrow will show you where you need to go!*

10. *Traveling near or far, the way to protect your heart is to find a sheltered haven. So, to guard your dreams just remember by following your heart and saying your prayers…. they will ALL get you there.*

11. *If you are adrift, take charge of your ship, because if it crashes you will sink. To stay afloat steady your boat and in that choice redirection, making right decisions, you will not wreck, or go down below.*

12. *When you graduate BIG things will commence happening. So, don't ever be afraid to go a different way. Because as you begin again and start over, there will always be something good occurring today.*

13. *Graduating is like sliding or standing on thin ice. It will never be easy to face your future. But when you fall, pick yourself up. Finding your firm footing you will see that the future is not slipping on by.*

14. *Life and love should be celebrated hourly since that gift of time will Never again come your way! That's why you must Never take any night or day for granted. So, appreciate them all in a new way.*

15. *The act of mothering, sharing, and caring will always be important. So, whether you are a mother or not, don't forget to take care of others, and yourself… as you guard your family, home, and heart.*

16. *Painful, hollow day explosive memories will ruin life. That's why, to keep your days and nights safe inside your mind, you need to replace your detonating memories with sweet revitalizing possibilities.*

17. *Nothing can grow without pain. That means, no rose or person can bloom without hail. Therefore, know through pain you will get tougher as you grow, and being watered by the rain you will find hope.*

18. *By holding onto an Angel of the Heart you won't fall apart. So, to be happy find an uplifting person who has invisible wings, and as you bring them into your life, they will teach you to rise-up and sing.*

19. *Do you have an angel in life? The answer is yes if you have delight and insight. But if you haven't yet had an angel stay. Look for people who will bring a surprise to your day and a smile to your face.*

20. *The nice thing about moving on is finding the brighter, softer side of life. So, do not be frightened by hard scary times. Instead, put fear behind you and celebrate the best kind times that will soon arrive.*

21. *Take time to smile at the people you meet. And as you grin at those you greet; you will find that a smile will change Your life. Because finding a softer side of time, you will be happy and smiling inside.*

22. *Finding the right road won't be easy. In life there will be many Big potholes. But potholes are Nice, because when you slow down, potholes will show you the way to go, by keeping you on the Right side!*

23. *In your life, are you in the sunrise or sunset? Well that all depends on how much time you have left. So never knowing when you will be going away, be thankful, and joyful as you make the most of today.*

24. *No matter what you do wild storms will follow you. That's why you need to change your attitude! So, instead of seeing the pain in the rain, you need to see the beautiful rose that's growing and aging.*

25. *The fact is you Are cracking up! But it's how you come back from a fracture that matters. That's why when you have all you can take, fill in the cracks holding you back, with happiness, and laughter.*

26. *When you have had all you can take, stand up to the pain. And finding the way to stay whole inside your mind, by being strong, you will be able to face the fear, pain and lies that are messing up your life.*

27. *Is there a purpose to war? That all depends on what you are fighting for. So, to realize what you are fighting for in life, first find what plan, goal, or dream that's worth fighting for. Then fight for them.*

28. *To win the conflict know Who you are fighting. So, knowing you are in a battle for your happiness, peace, and life, call a truce on You! Then by Not Fighting With Your Mind, you will win the new fight.*

29. *Thank you, is never enough unless you say Thank You from the bottom of your heart! So, to protect your heart from falling apart find your start. Do the things that make you thankful, smile, and sparkle.*

30. *To be found do Not be missing in action. That means, to be located and seen you need to know who you are, also where you are going. Then being happy with Who you are, nothing will ever be missing.*

31. *To not run out of time, don't be left behind. To finish what you started, know that the situation and work are done. Next to finish the job as more time comes, be ready to start and finish the next one.*

JUNE

Joslinfitzgerald.com

*To find the EXCITING SURPRISES waiting inside, Click
on the QR CODES that have been provided.
There you will see that these lighthouse guides will take you where you need to go!*

1. *At your breaking point are you breaking apart, breaking away, breaking into, or breaking out. That depends on what is involved in the breakup. So, to keep it together in all ways don't break down today.*

2. *When things break up, fall apart, and sadly end… remember to Mourn their loss. Then starting over again, spend the rest of your time enjoying your new morning and celebrating your life's next start.*

3. *To keep from feeling lost, adrift, and untethered find your fresh purpose in life today. Surviving your turning-points you will discover the perseverance and new direction you need that will come your way.*

4. *To fill your nest with hope, first know what your nest is made of. Because you will either be happy at home, or sadly alone. So, to find what You are made of, don't question life, your purpose, or goals.*

5. *When you are worried don't concentrate on depressing moments. Instead, to end your stress and heal your body, as you refresh your mind, always look forward to the better times that will soon be arriving.*

6.   *To be safe stop slipping through the cracks, then take a step back. When you realize giving things a second chance is a good idea by not falling apart and staying focused you will find balance just in time.*

7.   *If it hasn't happened yet, it's NOT bad news. So, do not be disturbed by sad things coming, until they happen. Don't expect the worst. Look forward to things getting better, by making your own good news!*

8.   *From nest to rest to keep from cracking up you need to hold it together. In life you have two choices, you can crack up and fall apart. Or by Not giving up as you keep moving on you will be going forward.*

9.   *The waiting game can be depressing, so to find rest, stop waiting for things to come your way. Go out and get them. Don't wait for things to change. Change them. Then following clues life will change you.*

10.   *Everything in time is about waiting in line. You will either be first or last depending on how the line moves. But last-minute decisions that have to do with keeping you moving… will be found as you Wait.*

11.   *Falling through the cracks is not bad. It just means you have been going the wrong cracked up way. Now realizing your oversight, pick yourself up. Then by not cracking apart, you will find the right path.*

12.   *To escape you must first be locked up. To break the lock as you release the stress holding you back, Break out. Do not break down. Then releasing your mind, you will be able to survive your hard times.*

13.   *To keep from cracking up, let up on yourself. Be nice to you! Don't doubt your plans or what you want to do. And as you escape indecision and become sure of choices, you will have less apprehension.*

14. *To find the light open your eyes. And that's good insightful advice, because if you stay blind to what is right in front of your eyes, as you fall for lies, you will never survive the facts-of-life or see the light.*

15. *Why do you hide from the answers when you know that they are right? In life you must hear things accurately and See things clearly. So, to never be blindsided you need to trust your directional insight.*

16. *To find serenity listen to the lullaby in your mind, then you will be able to find your delight inside. Next knowing optimism and extra courage will guard your heart, that's when the real music will start.*

17. *To make sure the last song is not sung, keep singing! And as you sing your songs remember to live a long life is easy. All you need to do is keep your heart beating, while enjoying life, and breathing.*

18. *To know someone is watching over you, look around. And in that clue you will see, as you want nice things for those in your life, there will always be kind cool people who want good things for you too.*

19. *To sing a song of love, first Love Yourself. But know it's not your face that makes you attractive or charming it's Who you are, what's inside your heart, and what you do for others, that sets you apart.*

20. *To keep from being blindsided listen to all sides. You always need to consider all parts of a question. And as you do, while thinking it through, in the middle of review, you will find your new redirection.*

21. *Are you scared of running out of time? It's not time you should dread. It's Wasting time that brings tears and will mess with your head. So, stop throwing time away and make the most of your day ahead.*

22. *To make the most of the past, don't run out of time. And as the past fades away, enjoy the sentences you will be writing today. Because today will become the next chapter's title of your life's frontpage!*

23. *Walking on the tombstone line, heed the warning signs. They will turn you around just in time. So, to go the right way listen to*

what the caution lights say and as you stop trouble you will survive the day.

24. *Dreaming is like letting your mind take flight. That's why to enjoy the wild ride of life everyday you must reach for the sky. Then knowing your goals can come true, your future will be revealed to you.*

25. *Do you want to rise over the mess and fly away from stress! Knowing flying is not possible. To find stability, keep your feet on the ground. Face your stress so you can clean up what's bringing you down.*

26. *To get ready know where you are going. To find purpose when you get there you need to realize that even if life is a rocky road, going in the right direction, there will always be a reason to sing as you go.*

27. *Hanging around getting ready to go, know what you are doing. Learning your life lessons realize even if the road was full of potholes, there was a good reason for those bumps, doubts, and blow outs.*

28. *Are you in the dark? Has sight lost its delight? Have your goals fallen apart? Is that how you want to spend time? If not, open your eyes. Don't let the dark planned plots inside your heart ruin your life.*

29. *To keep from being lost and alone you need to find your way back home. Therefore, to find where you belong follow your heart. By trusting your open heart, you will never be forlorn, drifting, or lonely.*

30. *To find your way out of the perfect storm you need to see the piloting light on the other side. So, to end your imprisonment, and to get through your life, you need to find your strength and bliss inside.*

June's Surprise Writing. In life everybody is always thinking about time. Thats why, knowing we are all running out of time we need to realize, if we don't fear the changes in time, as we see the passing of time as a good thing… Time will always be a good friend in our life.

JULY

Joslinfitzgerald.com

*To find the EXCITING SURPRISES waiting inside, Click
on the QR CODES that have been provided.
There you will see that these lighthouse guides will take you where you need to go!*

1. *No ride in life is free. Every ride comes at a price. So, to find the prize and surprise in your timeline, even though life comes at a high price, seek serenity, peace, and release inside your heart that Is free.*

2. *To take flight in your mind find liberty, freedom, resolution, and compromise. To seek your escape in time, release yourself from bad things in life. Don't let pain, of today take away the hope of tomorrow.*

3. *To experience freedom be free inside your mind. Don't let the problems of today weigh you down and take away your smile. Enjoy your plans, reach for your opportunities, and don't fear your time or life.*

4. *Do you feel like a firework exploding in a million pieces? With things falling apart tests, depression, and messes will lead to many challenges. So, for your mind to find freedom put your life back together.*

5. *Liberty means many things. But to find freedom from your problems you must know what it means to you. So, to find celebration inside your mind, do not fear what's happening on your tombstone line.*

6. *People who play with dynamite will see life blow up. Therefore, don't let explosive angry things come your way. Instead focus on*

goodwill also relaxation and don't let things blow up in your face today.

7. *Breathing is free! For other things lost there will be a cost. So, don't let the burden of what you lost and left behind take a high price on life. Breathe and know satisfaction and contentment are coming.*

8. *Dreams must burn bright or die! If a dream dies it will be like an incinerated firecracker exploding in a flash of time. That's why to Not burn out or give in keep your dreams alive, don't give up on them.*

9. *To avoid the burn out in life put out the fire. Don't run away. Put out the flames of indecision. Don't doubt yourself. And once you make your choice stand by it, follow it through. Don't give up on you!*

10. *In life you will feel like pain is keeping you down. So, to get the old load off your shoulders try to find a Bright side of time and don't let nervousness or nightmares take away your slice of paradise.*

11. *To keep your dreams from burning down and going up in smoke, don't let your old goals incinerate. Dreams and goals are the same. So set your goals release your heart and stop burning up your dreams.*

12. *To find light in the night you must have sight, or your dreams will soon take flight. So, keep your goals, plans, and ideas in sight, don't let them fly by. Don't let your goals, dreams, ideas, and plans die.*

13. *To end the stress of your wild ride let your troubles and problems die. To find paradise in life, don't fill your days with hate, sadness, pain, or lies. Decide to live with happiness, peace, and enlightenment.*

14. *Don't be afraid of things you can't see. Instead put your fear of the unknown away and conquer the things you Can perceive. Then finding life can be a version of paradise, things won't be so frightening.*

15. *To survive the bumpy ride hold on tight to what is right. Sadly, life will be a frightening wild ride. That's why you need to be a good driver, so you can drive around the potholes that are in your sight.*

16. *To have sweet dreams. You must know fear wears many faces. Fear will be found in all places. But fear can go away. So, to protect your nice heart from what will tear it apart defeat fear with confidence.*

17. *To stop falling know what you are falling for. To survive the tricks and lies never fall for the things that make you cry. Instead fall in love with life! Then you will know how to survive the hard times!*

18. *The ride in life will be nice when you learn to drive. So, to make sure you head the right way, obey the stop signs, and red lights, take it slow. Then when you get a green light, you will be ready to Go!*

19. *On life's wild ride hold on tight. Because if you lose your grip there will be more fright than delight. The fact is hard times and struggles will arrive, but following your plans and goals, you can survive.*

20. *To avoid the disappointment of failure, go to the softer side of your mind. So, when you are ready to give up, keep on going, because success, contentment, and the desires of your heart are yet to come.*

21. *In planning for your roller coaster future, doors will open, others will close. That's why, if old doors close, that is a good thing! Because finding a new way to go, not all doors are meant to be opened.*

22. *To seek the light inside means you found sight. That's important to realize, because to see things clearly you need to depend on insight and wisdom so your direction and objectives will be well-defined.*

23. *To be full of intelligence means you figured out a way to answer your questions and feed your mind. So, to learn from your life lessons, as the student becomes the teacher, you will soon survive your trial.*

24. *Bad things happen all the time, so we can appreciate the good things in life! That's why you need to realize when something bad happens there will be good times coming after that old shattering disaster.*

25. *To keep your heart from breaking apart, do not get to your breaking point. Don't let others control your unpredictable temper. Trust what is right, by finding peace in your mind, then End your anger.*

26. *To stop crying all the time, dry your eyes. When you feel like everything is falling apart, trust your ideas. Then your thoughts also abilities will give you the cease-fire, and the assistance you are seeking.*

27. *Our sweet childhood memories are like wine hanging on the vine. So, any time being an adult is too hard, find the good times inside your mind. Then becoming a child again, go back to a nicer kind time.*

27. *To enjoy Any-time in life, the past, present, and future must fall in line. So, realizing in different ways every month is the same, means you can find reconciliation, purpose, support, and success daily.*

29. *Life will bring terror and serenity. That's why to replace fright with delight, look for the nice things in sight. Then Not running out of time, by leaving fear behind, you will find what makes you smile.*

30. *Insight found in your mind can shine a light into the blackest night. So, don't suffer the blindness of life. Have a positive outlook. Then having a healthy attitude, you will See things through clear eyes.*

July's Surprise Writing. With the times in your life Rearranging. Realizing there are some of you who are not seeing these changes as good things. Likewise realizing that there are some of you who are not finding any reason to be celebrating. If you want to have fireworks day and night, I have news for you. Because if you want to find the best things in life, that kind of negative attitude needs to change today! That's why, to be happy even when you want to cry, you need to remember even as you are struggling with hardships day and night, if you are peaceful and calm inside your mind, there will always be something good and sweet to celebrate all the time.

AUGUST

Joslinfitzgerald.com

To find the EXCITING SURPRISES waiting inside, Click
on the QR CODES that have been provided.
There you will see that these lighthouse guides will take you where you need to go!

1. *In summer's last call the season will turn into fall. So, knowing you can't keep time from fluctuating. Enjoy fall! And as you enjoy the changes inside, you won't be afraid of falling, or fear what is coming.*

2. *To find the reason for Once Upon a Time you need to locate your happily ever after in life. Then you will see the past and the present have each been colliding to make your future delightful and bright.*

3. *If you skip a beat, catch up! And from the beginning even though you are running behind, you will like your life. Because catching up with your desires, goals and plans means you are Not out of time.*

4. *For the lullaby of love to soothe you, you must know what the words mean. To find your happily now and ever after, you need to take care of you. You must love yourself, before you can fulfill your dreams.*

5. *Living on the tombstone line fill in your dots and dashes of time with the guidance you need to find. That end of the line thought, will guard your heart from the smash ups, and crashes that make you cry.*

6. *In life we are all leftover pieces of the lost frightened child hiding inside our mind. So, searching for stability and quiet we can't find, to not fall apart, let the past's kind history remain a part of your heart.*

7. *You don't have to know the words to listen to the music. Listening to the music of your heart you can write your own birth date, and a daily holiday song, if you take the time to slow down and sing along.*

8. *The only thing sweeter than cake is finding someone to share dreams with. So, to celebrate life and find the ones you trust, surround yourself with people who bring you inspiration, support, and love.*

9. *To enjoy a love song you must understand life. To celebrate your birthday, and favorite holiday every hour, next to never feel empty inside, share your time with somebody who you care about, also like.*

10. *In life there will be things you want yet cannot have. So, to be happy all the time don't worry about*

things you can't achieve. Instead appreciate what you have and those will be the things that you need.

11. *To find the difference between make-believe and reality give up on trusting sloppy kisses to grant your wishes. To believe in what's real know certainty will always be better than living a life of fantasy.*

12. *To make dreams come true know what you are searching for. To have a plan and stay true to your course, stay true to you. Then being happy with your decision you will find a new start will play its part.*

13. *To end disappointment and keep the party going find what makes you happy in life. Next to find the good news that makes you smile; you must be happy inside your mind. Make your own headline news!*

14. *To be wealthy, do you need riches un-told? No! So, in life don't worry about money, jewels, cars, or trophies. Instead, be content with what you have at home, knowing what you have is better than gold!*

15. *To find gladness in your heart make sure love never departs. To find love that stays, have patience, and endurance. So, take your time to do what is right, and know security will be found in a lovely life.*

16. *Is anyone really… happy? Only you can make you happy! So, Love yourself for who you are. Don't worry about who others think you should be, or what they want you to do. Just be happy being you!*

17. *The seasons will create chaos. That's why, to survive the destruction in life when you pick up the left-over pieces know damage brings rebuilding. Then you will see starting over is a part of transformation.*

18. *Do you ever worry you are Not in the right place, doing the right thing, at the right time? Well guess what, you are Right where you are supposed to be. So Don't doubt the timetable in your story's history.*

19. *Don't worry about your life, you will eventually get it right. So, now just relax and enjoy your new time. To find the delight in a troubled night don't cry, and enjoy your dreams, that dance in your mind.*

20. *Birds use wild winds to lift them safely above storms, tornadoes, and hurricanes. So, on your way to who you will be, to survive your problems use what you Know to lift you over your life's wild tornados.*

21. *If you want to see who cares for you? You must first care for someone too. Therefore, to end your selfish story, you need to put others first. And as you care more for them, they will care more for you too.*

22. *Have you ever felt trapped with no way out? To release yourself from your sinking conflict, realize when you replace your doubt, with clarity, as you follow your exit path, there is always a way out.*

23. *Feeling like a puppet in life and pawn of love, are you letting someone pull your strings and make your decisions. If so, take charge of life, cut the strings, don't take the bait, don't let them run your day.*

24. *In life is it better to be nice to others, or for others to be nice to you? Well guess what both of those insights are a part of the Golden rule. Because when you are nice to others, others will be nice to you.*

25. *With summer turning into fall, a trade-off will arrive. That's why, to enjoy your last call, and not fall victim to fear, pain or The Fall. Appreciate every night also day that comes your way as time calls.*

26. *In life you will be sad or mad. But people who made or Make you like that, won't remember what they did. So, if they can forgive and Forget you can too. Don't let the past take away your happy future.*

27. *One day a tornado, or hurricane of life will call your name. So, Never knowing when devastating storms will come your way, look for the good in change. And finding the rainbow, Don't fear the hail!*

28. *Have you been in a tornado or seen the damage on TV a hurricane brings? Like life hurricanes and tornados are frightening. But after the damage there will be delight in the restoration, and renovation.*

29. *Hurricanes, Tornados, and pain are the same. So, knowing pain is the same, no matter its name, to survive any kind of destruction, know there will be a great transformation when the devastation is over.*

30. *You Can survive the disasters in life. So, if you get hit by a fire, hailstorm, earthquake, hurricane, or tornado, seeing the grass turn green after the damage, your home, heart, and hope will be restored.*

31. *Life will be a wild ride! That's why to survive more pain than you think you can take, find the calm thoughts inside you. Then leaving yesterday's frightening agony behind look forward to better times.*

August's Surprise Writing. Is time your enemy or friend? Well that all depends on how you treat time as you are going around bend. So, to make sure time will always be your friend, Don't treat time like it is an enemy! Instead look forward to the time that is….as you also look forward to the time that has yet to be. Then searching for the best that has yet to be…. time will no longer be your enemy.

SEPTEMBER

Joslinfitzgerald.com

To find the EXCITING SURPRISES waiting inside, Click
on the QR CODES that have been provided.
There you will see that these lighthouse guides will take you where you need to go!

1. *As the seasons Fall in line people get sick, hurt, some die. Time will change your life. But know those things did not happen to you! You are still healthy also alive. So don't stop living and enjoy your life!*

2. *To survive the pain that will drive you insane find your safe place. To find your safe place, face what's bothering you. And as you stand up to worry, by not running away from trouble, stress will disappear.*

3. *In life there will be floods of trouble that bring dark waters and trying times. But as the storms subside, and the light arrives, knowing hope comes with tomorrow, today there will be peace inside your mind!*

4. *Who you are calling, as you are falling depends on what you are falling for! So, to find your shield of protection don't fall for the new destructive things coming your way. Don't let your any anxiety stay.*

5. *When treasurers become trash nothing lasts. So, to make sure that your treasures do not become trash, treasure all your days. Then finding hope and riches in tomorrow, don't let the good times fade away.*

6. *To see the morning's glory, find the light inside your eyes. To stop hiding, keep going, and know by leaving the past behind… in*

the morning, there will be no mourning, if you celebrate the new sunrise.

7. *A flood will wipe away every-Thing in life. But after the water recedes you will find that the buried seeds will grow. So, knowing that old floods of trouble will be over, look for the rose to bring you hope.*

8. *To survive the pain that drives you insane don't let fear control your days. Next turning your back on what makes you unhappy, find safety in your mind. Heal yourself inside. Don't let fear drive you crazy.*

9. *You can't keep away from problems or ignore discouragement. So, face what's bothering you. And as you end your stress, by cleaning up your mess, you will see the end to your lingering testing depression.*

10. *To stay out of harm's path pass your tests. To survive the mess as you learn from your mistakes fix your slipups. By learning your life lessons keep your heart safe, and you will stay out of worries way.*

11. *Do not live life like a dying lily. Do not focus on devastation, or destruction. Instead, know a seed will grow as it follows its goals! And like a strong seeded rose concentrate on your growth as you go.*

12. *To understand the autumn wind you need to know boring days and routine seasons have a beauty about them. So, enjoy the ordinary days that will soon begin, no matter which season of life you are in.*

13. *Before the last call you need to realize that Problems are the Teachers of life. So, to understand why life still feels like a classroom full of rules.... appreciate your Teachers, they have a lot to reveal to you.*

14. *With No warning at all before you lose the fall days, there will be a last call to enjoy the change. So, knowing change can be a good thing, don't run away from progress. Don't fear what transforms you.*

15. *You need to chase your plans and dreams, or you will lose your mind and the game. So, remember, to play ball no matter what the game is you are playing, your goals and dreams will always be waiting.*

16. *To avoid disappointments as you play the games of life you won't always be able to win. But having a strong, positive attitude every day you will be a winner in your dreams even if you lose everything.*

17. *To realize its good news, trust good news is coming. To be on the winning team know you can win the game. To be happy, put the bad news and losing attitudes behind you. Then find your good news!*

18. *To stop the fire put out the flames. To take away the disappointment of losing, know how to win the game. To fix your problems know what first caused your trouble and pain, then you won't do that again.*

19. *To make the right decision keep your eye on the ball. And being on the ball, while not dropping the ball, as you hold it all together, you will find that you Do have the balls to play and win the ball game.*

20. *To survive the changes in your life, even if those changes bring heartache, desolation, and pain you must realize change will always be a good thing. Because change will constantly take you in a new way.*

21. *To understand seasons of life find the reason for the end and beginning of time. And as everything old stops, and new starts, as old becomes new again that will give you a reason to enjoy the transitions.*

22. *To follow the teaching signs that lead to peace and prosperity know another year is fading away. To find the best in your day seek beauty in each season and appreciate the life lessons that come your way.*

23. *In life everybody is always thinking about time. That's why knowing we are all running out of time, we need to realize, if we don't fear the changes in time, that time will always be a good thing in our life.*

24. *To keep things from going south, stay on the right route. And if you are going the wrong way, and your hopes, dreams also goals are dying today, Hold on Tight! Your plans will know the right way to go.*

25. *To tell if things are beginning or ending know deep down inside as you survive the stormy facts-of-life that things will get better. So, as you get stronger, always know that your stop is just another start.*

26. *Going around the bend to see if someone is an enemy or friend depends on how you treat them. To make friends out of the people, who don't like You. Be nice to them! Don't treat people like enemies.*

27. *Like life, the weather and seasons will turn overnight. So, knowing things will end, you must be ready for what the new start brings. Then, looking forward to the beginning, you will find the best of everything.*

28. *Do not let fear or pain change your day, remember frightening things will soon go away. So, focus on what's good in life. Then let the bad thoughts, and destructive things leave your mind and sight.*

29. *When you are caught in a half and half trap, you will need to find an escape from your cage. So, knowing that things will get better. Don't let depression, indecision, or devastation keep you locked away.*

30. *Do you need a vacation from life? A trip from tests and problems would be nice. But, knowing that break can't happen! Stop stressing about old decisions and take a refreshing mental break vacation.*

September's Surprise Writing. To make sure every day is a reason to celebrate, you need to remember your day is not beautiful because it's new. Instead, Your day is beautiful, because as you change your bad, sad, fearful attitude, and create the happy, rejuvenating sights in your life, there is a New You!

OCTOBER

Joslinfitzgerald.com

To find the EXCITING SURPRISES waiting inside, Click
on the QR CODES that have been provided.
There you will see that these lighthouse guides will take you where you need to go!

1. As harvest starts and fall calls while things are getting tricky. Don't forget no matter how life taunts and haunts you, to survive the after math of a trick, you need to find the treat and peace in the season.

2. Do you want what you should not have? Or do you want to receive what you need! Remember what you want will not always be good for you. But receiving what you need will complete and fulfill you!

3. As the seasons change, and life changes, to make sense of Change, stay strong. Do not be afraid of things changing or trading places. To survive the trick of starting over keep going and enjoy exploring.

4. In life's tricky season have you ever felt like the only leaf on the tree? Feeling alone is not the way life should be. So, to make a new Friendly tree stay away from people who want you to be sad or lonely

5. To find out who you will be, what you need to be doing, and where you are going, make sure you are going the right way, doing what you should be doing. Then you will like the person you end up becoming.

6. To stop the following black shadow that's dark as night. End the hesitancy in your life. To eliminate the doubtful, sneaky, creepy

things that hold you back, let your light shine, by taking off your mask.

7. *Are you negotiating with someone about something? Well to survive the trick, and find the treat, stop letting others scare you into doing wrong things! Instead take charge of your right terrific decisions.*

8. *To keep from being trapped, find the way out. To locate the way to make half and half whole when life seems hollow find a way to escape and plug up the hole. Don't get trapped in an old, trapped gap.*

9. *The difference between a trick or treat, one is sweet, other creepy. So, if you are stuck in the middle of a big decision put the tricks behind you. Find the smart, sweet things in life that don't scare you.*

10. *With someone trapped in a nightmare, it takes one smile to change a life. So, never knowing what depression somebody is in remember a smile and kind word lets them know someone cares about them.*

11. *The sweet treats in life are easy to find if you slow down and take your time. So, to avoid icky tricks and tricky traps don't take the wrong path. Make smarter choices that bring the sweet things back.*

12. *To know if you are going the right way you must know which way you are heading. So, to know which way you need to go, find the difference between giving up, and slowing down. Then keep going!*

13. *To survive spooky times know a smile given away will bring hope into someone's day. So, realizing caring will never be scary, to keep someone breathing, share your healing love with everybody you see.*

14. *In life to know if you are a leaf or tree, know if you are strong or weak. To change the days in your life, look inside and realize you are not a dying leaf. Instead, you are a sturdy durable ever green tree.*

15. *To have life be whole not hollow, also to find what lasts, you must stop living in the past. Sadly, the past is full of sad hollow holes. But the hope of tomorrow will keep you whole because it is wide open.*

16. *To be evergreen inside your heart and serene inside your mind shows you found the way to love life. That's why, as you keep living, to stay evergreen, think clearly, so you can keep growing and going.*

17. *What does evergreen mean and why is it important to your life? Evergreen means even when your plans die, if you are evergreen and peaceful inside, that your hopes, goals, and desires will stay alive.*

18. *Haunted by the past to stay away from the tricks in life you must find the reason for their deception. So, Don't let the treacherous past trick you into thinking it is your future. Don't let the bad past last!*

19. *Living in a haunted house of doubt to keep from falling for tricks you need to avoid ones that make you sick. So, close the door on dishonesty. Then being truthful with yourself… life will figure itself out.*

20. *The difference between Hello and Hell-no is coming or going. That's why to survive the icky tricks if you are asking if Hell is real. While facing the fire, to not burn up! You should not try to find out!*

21. *Things are getting tricky. So, to know what is close, you need to see the trick coming! Next, to avoid tricks in life that make you sick outside and inside, stay away from the things that hurt and panic you.*

22. *Are you wondering who keeps playing tricks on you? Well Guess What, that's You! So, to stay away from tricky icky thoughts that cause you to doubt your future in some way. Stop tricking yourself today.*

23. *To avoid the sick tricks you keep playing on yourself. Stop tricking your mind into thinking things are fine. Instead, to make things fine, find the renewal and repair that makes you healthy and wise.*

24. *To elude the ruse and find truth decide if it is the trick or sweet treat you seek. To see the difference between a trick or treat, turn your back on misery, start living. Find the plan that will become the treat.*

25. *Knowing sick tricks will be news. You must know what a lie is, and what is truth. So, to see through the tricky trap, turn your back on bad news. Do not believe lies. Only let reliable news direct your life.*

26. *To hang on as the world goes around, find a way to keep your feet on the ground. So, to stop Booing and Yelling about what is happening, to keep from falling apart, celebrate the good that will soon start.*

27. *Are you a part of the Booing Disgusted group like most are. To know why you are Booing, you must stand up to what is upsetting you. To do something about what disgusts you, Fix it and stop Boooooing.*

28. *Are you hiding behind your mask afraid to let people see what you conceal inside? Take off your mask! Let your smile shine. Then no longer hiding they will see the good things going on in your mind.*

29. *What do you want to be for Halloween? Who do you want to be in life? Yes those are good inquiries because a costume will not be as important as the kind unmasked person who the people see and like.*

30. *Don't scare kids. That's good advice day or night. Because no matter our age, we are still terrified kids in life. So, to dry our tears we need to find a way to escape fear, by not letting terror come near.*

31. *Lift up your mask that you are hiding behind, so you can see things clearly and easily. Then, doing to others as you want them to do to you the golden rule is a good place to know what you need to do!*

October's Surprise Writing. With Falls full orange moon chorus lifting up over the horizon. Realizing we would all love to have a reason to celebrate and sing songs every day. You need to remember you don't have to know the words to listen to the music play. Because listening to the music of your heart, by finding the harmony inside your mind. As your suns keep rising, you can write your own uplifting and inspiring songs… as long as you take the time to slow down and sing along.

NOVEMBER

Joslinfitzgerald.com

To find the EXCITING SURPRISES waiting inside, Click
on the QR CODES that have been provided.
There you will see that these lighthouse guides will take you where you need to go!

1. Coming into the month of Thanksgiving remember as we celebrate freedom, peace, and many other liberating things, every day from beginning to the ones in-between will be a time of Thanks and giving.

2. Something big is coming. So, to find the good news know if something is true or false. Then verifying the variation between right, wrong, good, or bad you will know what you are Thankful for in your life.

3. Do you know the reason for Thanksgiving? Here is a clue, it does not have anything to do with pies, turkey, or sides. Instead, Thanksgiving has to do with everything good and nice You see and say in life.

4. To know what you are Thankful and grateful for every day and night, You need to have something, also somebody in life you are grateful for and Thankful to. Yes, that includes being Thankful for You!

5. There's a lot to be Thankful for. So, no matter what good or bad things keep happening, you need to be Thankful for Everything. Because just living, loving, and breathing are miracles, and true blessings.

6. *To understand Thanksgiving, and to know what time it is, appreciate the time you have been given. In life as you breathe, hear, taste, smell, touch, love, and see, be Thankful for your seasons and senses.*

7. *To find the survival supplies you need in life, you need to realize that every night and day, for every reason, of every season is a gift of time for you to find something to be truly Thankful for in all ways.*

8. *What is on your Thanksgiving list? Yes, that should be an easy silent reply. Because knowing you are alive, everything good and nice in your life, is something that you should be Thankful for all the time.*

9. *Is it better to give or receive, in many ways they are the same. Because if you give happiness and love you will receive it back. And if you receive the same, you will have more to love and happily give away.*

10. *To be Thankful for what you receive, you must give unconditionally. That means, giving to others who are in need, you and those who have received, will each be blessed and thankful for that nice deed.*

11. *To give Thanks you must know what you are Thankful for. Shore to shore that truth has everything to do with being Thankful for family, friends, jobs, health, home, You, your life, and oh so much more.*

12. *To be truly Thankful every day in some way, say Thank You to someone in your life, including the people teaching you lessons you don't like. Being educated you will find the blessings you are seeking.*

13. *To be grateful for what you received don't concentrate on what you're missing! Instead, be thankful for everything! That means you need to appreciate that you are still breathing and enjoy your seasons.*

14. At the end of a cough, sneeze, or wheeze be Thankful you are still living. To know if someone cares if you are breathing and healing you must care for the people who will always be part of your recovery.

15. Don't fear your cough, wheeze, or sneeze. That just means you are fearful of living and breathing. Instead, to find your peace don't fear what's happening, and look forward to the good things coming.

16. The difference between Thanks and misery depends on how you look at things. So, to be abundantly happy don't live in a world of sadness, instead enjoy your joyful days of Thanksgiving and gladness.

17. Does anybody out there really care for you? Well to know that they do; you must care for people too. Then as you show them you care; You will appreciate the people who are there caring and loving you.

18. To know the meaning of Thanksgiving, start at the beginning. Looking forward to the end, do not fear the future. Then knowing the true blessing is in the Middle, you will be grateful for Everything!

19. To be Thankful you must know the difference between agitation and elation. Because when you can see the real blessing is in your Daily Celebration that's when you will really understand Thanksgiving!

20. To prepare for the feast be ready for what is set in front of you. That's why to enjoy the sides and pies, as you stop crying and drinking wine, you need to realize that the best has yet to come in your life.

21. To know what to be thankful for stop whining and crying about what you don't have. To understand Thanksgiving, you need to appreciate what you have already received and what gifts are still arriving.

22. To know if your plate is full or empty is important. Because if life is empty your heart will never be full. So, fill your life with nice things and kind thoughts and a lot of love, then you will be full of it All.

23. To know what Thanksgiving is, give others around you a Reason to be thankful you are in their life. To know what you are being fed and are thankful for, fill life with pleasure, expectation, and optimism.

24. When you give something away with a grateful heart that you already received, you will be blessed daily. Then being kind and nice to others in some way that will make every day a Thankful holiday.

25. Black Friday means many things. But it should never mean that any day in-between, ever has black clouds or will be unhappy. So, to keep a silver lining in life leave darkness and disappointment behind.

26. Are things in short supply? If so that's too bad, because that means things are missing in your life. So, to make sure nothing is missing in your time you need to be Thankful for what you have received.

27. Things in life will come at a high price, and sometimes you can't pay the extreme cost. But even so, daily know, when you can't pay the price, love, peace, breathing, and enthusiasm will always be free!

28. To make everyday a date to Celebrate something, you need to know what you're Thankful for. To be Thankful for everything in your life you need to realize Every date is a time to Celebrate Everything!

29. To know if it is over, first know why it started. Then in the beginning you will know how to finish it. Next when you know how to finish what you started, you will be able to Celebrate and begin again!

30. Every revealed hour, you get one moment closer to knowing who you are, also who you want to be! That means this year you are one Second nearer to being more Thankful and Grateful for Everything!

DECEMBER

Joslinfitzgerald.com

*To find the EXCITING SURPRISES waiting inside, Click
on the QR CODES that have been provided.
There you will see that these lighthouse guides will take you where you need to go!*

1. It's time to start wrapping things up. This includes wrapping up presents, fears, tears, and the year. But as you are Wrapping up Time, don't wrap up the present of the Present, that will be coming near.

2. To know the reason for the season realize what you need to find. In that reason for any season after you find what you are looking for, you will see the present is the Present of life, forevermore, and time.

3. To enjoy the beginning… work towards a Happy ending. To be content at the ending, look forward to your Presents present. So be clear, to be full of good cheer go into the New Year without fears or tears!

4. To find the difference in your life between crying and smiling, you need to realize that Christmas has nothing to do with what's inside a present. Instead Christmas IS the Present of the Present, that has just come near…and Time is the gift of the New Year!

5. To make sure Christmas is Not about buying, selling, and presents. Know the gift of your present is what the Present, and future will be giving. So, enjoy your Present's present because Living is the gift.

Merry Christmas!

6. *Is it better to be given presents in your Present? Or to know the Present is your present. That depends on if you know the difference between the Present and present, also the present of the Presents Future.*

7. *At Christmas you will receive presents and gifts you will exchange, break, or put away. But there is one life-changing gift you should always treasure and keep, that is the Present of your present today!*

8. *The way you say things matters. The things you do are important too. So, today and in any season be careful what you say, because what you say, and how you do it, really does matter, to others and to you.*

9. *With the past changing into the future. At the end, going into a beginning, you must find the present of the Present that will last. So, to be happy in your future, Don't Look For Your Present In The Past!*

10. *To follow The Star know what you are seeking and why you need to find it. In that pursuit You also need to know differences between a star, star, and The Star, so you know what you are searching for.*

11. *Before you open your mouth control your sharp cutting tongue. Keeping your annoying unpleasant words to yourself, you will be happier with who you are. That will be a present for you and everyone!*

12. *To find the Star of your heart realize that is a great present. Next to know the difference between a present and the Present you must First find the present of the Present in your past and new start.*

13. *The difference in the past or future is looking forward to something or sending it away. To make sure mistakes of your past don't follow you into your future, take care of the Presents present, today!*

14. *Finding the light in your life will always be important if you want to get out of the dark. That's why you first need to be your own guiding light so you can be the lighthouse light in somebody else's life.*

15. *To be a wise person know how to be a wise man! To be a wise man, even if you are a woman, means you understand what it is to be wise. So, to be wise no matter who you are, find the best things in life.*

16. *Searching for something, know Where you need to find it. Finding it, know Why it was important. That's great insight because searching, finding, and knowing what you are looking for change's lives.*

17. *To have the perfect homecoming your heart must first find a place where it can go home. So, on your journey of love to be happy in life you must find the place where your heart and mind want to go.*

18. *Is there a difference between a shepherd and king? No there is not! They both take care of their herd and flock. So, if you are rich or poor protecting your friends and family they all need you equally.*

19. *You celebrate big events, but overlook small things, and that's not right. So, remember you won't have anything to celebrate if you don't appreciate the BIG little amazing things that make up your life.*

20. *The difference between Mourning and coming morning depends on if you are looking forward or backwards. So, stop Mourning the past. Look forward to the morning, which will end your Mourning.*

21. *Will you be home for Christmas? All depends on if you have a home to go to. And having a home all depends on you. That's why you need to know that your home will be found wherever your heart goes.*

22. *Why are trees important in your life? They are important because they mark the rings of time. So, knowing that in many ways you are like a tree. Make sure as time rolls on by that you keep growing.*

23. To know it's Not Santa coming around, you must know who has already come to town. That's why, to understand clauses in life you must read the fine print, so there won't be any mysteries or surprises.

24. T'was the night before Forevermore. And knowing Christmas will always be Every day like the day before. It's nice to know Forevermore, once again started this morning, as it has always done before.

25. Christmas means the most blessed time of the year is here! So, to enjoy each second of your present of the Present, as you receive your newest present, get ready to have a new Present and cool future too.

26. Christmas will never be over! Because Christmas and every holiday will always be every day. So, to find the greatest Present in Life, realize there will always be something great to Celebrate all the time.

27. To beat holiday stress, do not let desperation beat you down or beat you up. To defeat Depression, know Christmas is NEVER over. Because like love and hope, Christmas lives every day in your heart.

28. To cross the finish line and win the race do not run out of time. So, as the Old Year begins to end. And the New Year's Present prepares to begin find the best things in life by making Time Your Friend!

29. As the old year ends you can pretend things are okay, or you can face the reality that things need to change. So, knowing there are things that need Change, stop pretending they are okay. Change them!

30. Before you can wipe your slate clean you must know why it's dirty. So, take what you learned from the year, tidy time up. Next putting those dirty things and ugly thoughts behind you, clean up your life!

Merry Christmas!

DECEMBER 31

NEW YEARS EVE...

Knowing the last word said will always be the beginning of a "HAPPY NEW YEAR." Realizing that the last word heard has something to do with Time, Life, Survival, Hope, Renewal, Love, Guidance, Change, HAPPY, NEW, and YEAR. As the old year dies, and New Year arrives again, to enjoy the best of your past, and to appreciate the present of the Present.. You must realize the promise, of that new great, amazing, uplifting Future anticipation will always be leading you to A DAILY CELEBRATION!

And as you get ready to start your NEW YEAR here's one last thought that will make everything clear.

Have you ever felt like you are doing everything wrong? Have you ever felt like everybody else is doing something right! Well, here is some more great insight for you to celebrate day and night. And this Good News means there is absolutely nothing wrong with you!

You are just authoring your story a little slowly. You are filling in the pages of life more patiently, and you are seeing things more uniquely.

That's why as you take your time to figure things out, you will realize the difference between who you are, and who people want you to be... means you are a smart one-of-a-kind person who is just doing things a little bit differently. And that amazing truth will always take you to A Daily Celebration.

Now as your year has come to an end, and your NEW YEAR IS BEGINNING again. It is my prayer in your DAILY CELEBRATION OF LIFE that you will always have everything you want, like, and need, all the time. Likewise, as your plans Succeed, may you forever find safety, joy, and peace inside your heart and mind. Additionally, as you follow your Hopes, Goals and Dreams may you always have a HAPPY NEW YEAR coming! Next in the present of the Present while enjoying that Present of your present with the Gift of the Future arriving. Realizing that Happiness, Tranquility, and Freedom, are the Presents of your Present, and the Promise of your New Year that you need to tell others about, or that you need to receive. By finding the guidance you are seeking may you always have HAPPIER DAYS IN-BETWEEN!

Love and Blessings
Mary Fitzgerald Joslin...
Your Merry Author Joslin Fitzgerald

Information sheet

So, knowing Daily we will all be Celebrating SOMETHING in some-way. Realizing every hour will be something to CELEBRATE. TO FIND THE WAY TO BE HAPPY ALL OF YOUR LIFE. Let's take this time to appreciate the continuing gifts and blessings we have been given. And as, we look forward to the Present of the Todays Present, lets CELEBRATE the Happy Future coming our way.

NOW, TO READ THE POPULAR BLOG CALLED AWAY BACK HOME AND FOLLOW JOSLIN FITZGERALD'S WRITING, TO READ ALONG, PLEASE GO TO JOSLINFITZGERALD.COM

to find out about Joslin Fitzgerald's 18 bestselling children's books, 5 animated movies, Hollywood projects, and the exciting coming soon 15 adventure packed novels please visit her blog and web sites at JOSLINFUN.COM, or ARISINGWRITERS3.BLOGSPOT.COM or ARISINGWRITERS.COM

Published by Circles Legacy Publishing LLC
Book design copyright © 2023
TXU 2-393-849
Project Manager and Team Coordinator: Mary Cindell Lynn Pilapil
Cover Design: Jim Villaflores
Layout Coordinator: Joseph Apuhin

Published in the United States of America

ISBN: xxx-x-xxxx-xxxx-x

Adult Inspirational Journal
November 18, 2023